First World War
and Army of Occupation
War Diary
France, Belgium and Germany

16 DIVISION
Divisional Troops
Divisional Cyclist Company
18 December 1915 - 1 June 1916

WO95/1962/2

The Naval & Military Press Ltd
www.nmarchive.com
Published in association with The National Archives

Published by

The Naval & Military Press Ltd

Unit 10 Ridgewood Industrial Park,

Uckfield, East Sussex,

TN22 5QE England

Tel: +44 (0) 1825 749494

www.naval-military-press.com

www.nmarchive.com

This diary has been reprinted in facsimile from the original. Any imperfections are inevitably reproduced and the quality may fall short of modern type and cartographic standards.

© **Crown Copyright**

Images reproduced by permission of The National Archives, London, England, 2015.

Contents

Document type	Place/Title	Date From	Date To
Heading	WO95/1962 (2)		
Heading	16th Division 16th Divl Cyclist Coy. Dec 1915-Jun 1916		
Miscellaneous	The Officer Commanding 16th Divisional Cyclist Company.	29/10/1915	29/10/1915
Miscellaneous	16th. Divisional Cyclist Company	02/11/1915	02/11/1915
Miscellaneous	16 Co Formed 16 You 15		
Heading	16th Div. Cyclist Vol 1 Dec 18-31 Jan 16		
Heading	War Diary Of 16th Divisional Cyclist Company From 18th December 1915-To 31st January 1916 Volume I		
War Diary	Pirbright Pirbright Co. Surrey	18/12/1915	18/12/1915
War Diary	Southampton	18/12/1915	18/12/1915
War Diary	Le Havre	19/12/1915	20/12/1915
War Diary	Houchin	21/12/1915	23/12/1915
War Diary	Cite De Verquin	23/12/1915	31/01/1916
Heading	16th Cyclist Vol. 2		
Heading	War Diary Of 16th Divisional Cyclist Coy From 1st February 1916 To 29th February 1916 Volume II		
War Diary	Cite De Verquin	01/02/1916	14/02/1916
War Diary	Westrehem	15/02/1916	27/02/1916
War Diary	Busnes	28/02/1916	29/02/1916
Heading	War Diary Of 16th Divisional Cyclist Company From 1st March 1916 To 31st March 1916 Volume III		
War Diary	Busnes	01/03/1916	08/03/1916
War Diary	Hurionville	09/03/1916	26/03/1916
War Diary	Vaudricourt	27/03/1916	31/03/1916
War Diary	Noeux-Les Mines	31/03/1916	31/03/1916
Heading	War Diary Of 16th Divisional Cyclist Company From 1st April 1916 To 30th April 1916. Volume IV		
War Diary	Noeux-Les-Mines	01/04/1916	30/04/1916
Heading	War Diary Of 16th Divisional Cyclist Company From 1st May 1916 To 1st June 1916 (Inclusive) Volume V		
War Diary	Noeux-Les-Mines	01/05/1916	01/06/1916

Moss/1965 (2)

16TH DIVISION

16TH DIVL CYCLIST COY.
DEC 1915 - JUN 1916

I

The Officer Commanding,
16th Divisional Cyclist Company.

To enable me to comply with para 1930 King's Regulations 1912, please forward the following information:-

(i)   The Date of Formation of Company.

(ii) Any unusual means by which it was recruited or transfers received.

(iii) The Stations at which it was employed and the dates of its arrival at and departure from such Stations.

(iv) The Military operations in which it has been engaged, and its achievements.

(v)   The names of all officers killed and wounded, and the name of any officer or soldier who has specially distinguished himself in action.

(vi) Drafts received and despatched, their strength, dates of their arrival and departure and the names of officers who accompany them. Drafts numerically weaker than an Officer Party should not be separately specified.

(vii) Any other matter which may be considered of historical importance.

HOUNSLOW.   G. Maurice   Major for Colonel
29.10.15   I/C Army Cyclist Corps Records Hounslow.

II

From O.C. 16th D.C.C.
to O/C Cyclist Records.

I attach information upon the points enumerated above.

LIEUTENANT,
Adjutant, 16th Divisional Cyclist Company
for Capt. Comdg 16th D.C.C.

Pirbright Camp.
2/11/15

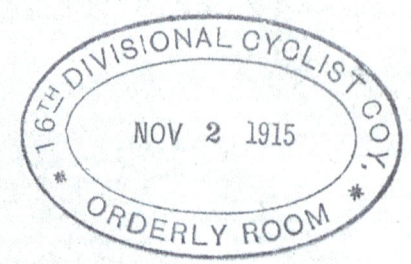

16th. DIVISIONAL CYCLIST COMPANY

(1) The Company was formed at MALLOW on the 16th. day of January 1915.

(2) The Company was composed of Officers, non-commissioned officers, and men drawn from the thirteen battalions of the 16th. (Irish) DIVISION.
At the date of formation its strength was that which was then the authorised establishment of a Cyclist Company, viz,--- 279. all ranks. During the spring and summer months of the year 1915 the strength was increased considerably by Recruits from Dublin, who were of a superior status; and on the 2nd of September 1915, the total strength being on that date 330 all Ranks: 72 N. C. Os. and Men were transferred to the 8th. Battalion Royal Inniskilling Fusiliers; leaving the Company 258. in strength. all Ranks.

(3) The stations at which the Company have been employed are as follows:---

        MALLOW.   16/1/15. to 15/4/15.

        BALLYVONARE. 15/4/15. to 18/6/15.

        BALLYHOOLEY. 18/6/15. to 7/8/15.

        FERMOY.   7/8/15. to 7/9/15.

        PIRBRIGHT.   8/9/15. to this date.

(4) Nil.
(5) Nil.
(6) Nil.
(7) Nil.

Pirbright Camp.
2/11/15.

(signature) LIEUTENANT,
Adjutant, 16th Divisional Cyclist Company
for Capt. Comdg. 16 D.C.C.

16 Co

Formed 16 Jan 15

Stationed Mallow
        Ballynovare
        Ballykooley
        Fermoy
        Pirbright

Left Southampton 18.12.15.
arr. France 19.12.15

19-1-16 Two men wounded.

Employed to 31.1.16 constructing trenches & other fatigue work.

16th Div. Cyclists
Vol 1

Dec 15-31
Jan '16

"Dec '15
Jan '16

Confidential

WAR DIARY
of
16th Divisional Cyclist Company
from 18th December 1915 – to 31st January 1916.

VOLUME I

W.W.Watson Capt.
Commdg 16th Divl Cyclist Coy.
31-1-16.

Army Form C. 2118.

WAR DIARY

~~INTELLIGENCE SUMMARY~~

(Erase heading not required.)

Instructions regarding War Diaries and Intelligence Summaries are contained in F. S. Regs., Part II. and the Staff Manual respectively. Title pages will be prepared in manuscript.

Place	Date	Hour	Summary of Events and Information	Remarks and references to Appendices
Pirbright PIRBRIGHT Co. SURREY	18/12/15	2·20 AM	The 16th Divisional Cyclist Company paraded for march to Brookwood station. Company Sergeant Major MURPHY_M.J. placed under arrest for drunkenness on this parade and left behind.	
		4·45 AM	The Company left BROOKWOOD station by train – Strength 8 Officers, 195 other ranks, 2 Horses L.D. one mule, one G.S. Limber wagon, one Cook's Cart, 203 cycles. Roll of officers:— Captain Lt. H. L. WATSON Commanding Officer " Lieutenant H. NEVILLE ROBERTS Second in Command " " A. Q. F. SIMMS ⎫ " 2nd Lieut. E. U. P. FITZGERALD ⎬ Platoon Commanders " " G. T. SHAW ⎪ " " G. M. E. BAYLY ⎪ " " J. HOGAN ⎪ " " S. GEDDES ⎭	
SOUTHAMPTON		6·45 PM	Arrived at SOUTHAMPTON.	
		6 PM	Left SOUTHAMPTON.	
LE HAVRE	19/12/15	4 AM	The Company arrived at LE HAVRE. (less transport party.)	
		8 AM	The Company transport arrived at LE HAVRE.	
		11 AM	The Company proceeded to the Rest Camp at LE HAVRE.	
		11 PM	The Company paraded for march to Railway Station.	
	20/12/15	3 AM	Left LE HAVRE.	
		11 PM	Arrived at FOUQUEREUIL (Ref. Map FRANCE, Sheet 36B, E.13) and there detrained.	
HOUCHIN	21/12/15	2 AM	Arrived at HOUCHIN (Ref. Map Sheet 36B, K.15) full strength, and billeted there.	

WAR DIARY

INTELLIGENCE SUMMARY.
(Erase heading not required.)

Army Form C. 2118.

Place	Date	Hour	Summary of Events and Information	Remarks and references to Appendices
HOUCHIN	22/12/15	2.30 P.M.	Sent one platoon to pull G.O.C's Car out of ditch. C.S.M. MURPHY rejoined under close arrest.	
	23/12/15	11.30 A.M.	Left HOUCHIN with orders to take over billets from 15th Div. Cyclist Coy in K.62 Map 36 B.	
CITÉ de VERQUIN	"	12 Noon	Arriving in K.62 Map 36 B. and took over billets of 15th D.C.C. in MINE Buildings K.5.d. and officers billets in CITÉ DE VERQUIN K.5.d. C.H.Q. in CITÉ DE VERQUIN, K.5.d.	
"	24/12/15		The Company commenced work on the fifth line of trenches, NOYELLES – SAILLY-LABOURSE, under direction of C.R.E. 45th Corps. Half Company worked daily at NOYELLES and (Ref. Map 36B. L.17.d.3.8 to L.12.d.3.2), and half Company on wiring trenches in L.9. Parade at 8 A.M. Cease at 3 P.M.	
"	25/12/15		Half Company at L.9 proceeded to work on trenches, NOYELLES. Start work at 9 A.M. owing to wet which made useful work impossible. Half Company at L.17.d did not proceed to work today, according to instructions of Engineers. One man sick, awarded by Divisional area.	
"	26/12/15		Half Company at L.17.d proceeded to work as usual. Half Company at L.9 did not proceed to work according to instructions of Engineers. Arrangement made with Engineers that five platoons will work each day, one platoon being retained in billets for guards, fatigues, etc. This platoon to be taken in rotation, and alternately from each half Company. The daily hours of work to be 9 A.M. to 3 P.M., with break of half an hour for food. These arrangements confirmed by B. General BUCKLAND, C.R.E. 45 Corps, in conversation with Second in Command, 16 D.C.C. today.	
"	27/12/15		Acting on orders of H.Q. 47th Division in whose billeting area the Company was billeted, the Company removed from the MINE Buildings into billets allotted by the 47th Div. along the main road BETHUNE – NOEUX-les-MINES in E.29.q. Æ E.30.c., two platoons being under canvas, two in barns, and two in Attics.	

[signature]

Army Form C. 2118.

WAR DIARY

INTELLIGENCE SUMMARY

(Erase heading not required.)

Instructions regarding War Diaries and Intelligence Summaries are contained in F.S. Regs., Part II. and the Staff Manual respectively. Title pages will be prepared in manuscript.

Place	Date	Hour	Summary of Events and Information	Remarks and references to Appendices
CITÉ DE VERQUIN	28/12/15		Work on trenches continued, and carried out daily as above specified, except and until such note as shall be made hereafter. Two sick men evacuated out of Divisional area.	
"	29/12/15 30/12/15 31/12/15		Nothing to record.	
"	1916 1/1/16	11 AM	C.S.M. MURPHY - M.J. tried by F.G.C.M. at HOUCHIN, on a charge "When on active service, drunkenness". One sick man evacuated out of Divisional area.	
"	2/1/16		Nothing to record. One man rejoined from hospital.	
"	3/1/16		B. General BUCKLAND, C.R.E. 4th Corps, in conversation with Second in Command 16th D.C.o., complimented the Company upon its excellent work done in the trenches. One sick man evacuated out of Divisional area.	
"	4/1/16		Three sick men evacuated out of Divisional area.	
"	5/1/16	x	Proceedings of F.G.C.M. in the case of C.S.M. MURPHY - M.J. Promulgated - Accused found guilty of the charge, and sentenced to be reduced to the ranks - Sergeant BAILEY. W. Promoted Company Sergeant Major vice C.S.M. MURPHY - M.J., to date from 18/12/15. (10 men sent as orderlies to 16th Div. Signal Coy H.Q. Section) Corporal KELLY. C.P. promoted Sergeant, vice Sergeant BAILEY. W. to date from 18/12/15. Private MOLONY - J. and DALY - J. appointed Paid Lance Corporals.	
"	5/1/16	x	4 sick men evacuated out of Divisional area.	

WAR DIARY

Army Form C. 2118.

Place	Date	Hour	Summary of Events and Information	Remarks and references to Appendices
CITÉ DU VERQUIN	7/1/16		Nothing to record.	
"	8/1/16		One man rejoined from hospital.	
"	9/1/16		Two men admitted to Hospital. One made evacuated, unfit for service.	
"	10/1/16		Three men admitted to hospital.	
"	11/1/16		One man " "	
"	12/1/16		One man Pneumonia out of Divisional Area. Four men rejoined from hospital.	
"	13/1/16		One man evacuated out of Divisional Area.	
"	14/1/16		One man rejoined from hospital.	
"	15/1/16		The following change were made in the working parties of the Company — 25 men proceeded to Trenches at Map 36b. G.26.a.3.0, and were employed daily upon laying tracks more Entanglements. The Remainder of The Company proceeded to MAZINGARBE - NOYELLES line from 36b L.17c. T.5. ⊘ to 36b L.17d. 7.4.8. 50 men proceeded to 36b G.26.a.3.0 and 36b. G.26.a.3.4.	
"	16/1/16		Remainder as on 15/1/16.	
"	17/1/16		Work as on 16/1/16.	
"	18/1/16		50 men Employed as on 16th and 17th, Remainder proceed to work at 36b L.24.c.2.8	
"	19/1/16		Work at Trenches as on 18/1/16, and continued until further notes.	

WAR DIARY
INTELLIGENCE SUMMARY

Army Form C. 2118.

Place	Date	Hour	Summary of Events and Information	Remarks and references to Appendices
CITÉ DE VERQUIN	19/1/16		Two men wounded by shell at 36 b. G.2.b.a.3.4., retained in hospital.	
"	20/1/16		One man admitted to hospital.	
"	21/1/16		Two men rejoined from hospital. Two men admitted to hospital.	
"	22/1/16		One man " " "	
"	23/1/16		One man rejoined from hospital.	
"	24/1/16		One man admitted to hospital.	
"	25/1/16		Nothing to record. Company resting.	
"	26/1/16		One man admitted to hospital. One L.D. Horse received in lieu of mule evacuated on 9/1/16	
"	27/1/16		One man admitted to hospital. 2 men rejoined from hospital. L.Cpl. Byrne B. promoted Corporal. – Pte Linhile C.C. appointed paid Lce Cpl. "One man " " "	
"	28/1/16		One man rejoined from hospital. Draft of nine men joined as reinforcements. 50 men working in MINX mines, unloading timber – remainder as usual.	
"	29/1/16		50 men " " " " "	
"	30/1/16		50 men " " " " " One man rejoined from hospital. One man " " " Work in MINX mines cancelled – Company all working as on 18/1/16 – and until further notice.	
"	31/1/16		One man admitted to hospital. – One man rejoined from hospital.	

16th Cyclists
Vol: 2

SECRET

WAR DIARY
of
16th Divisional Cyclist Co'y.

from 1st February 1916 to 29th February 1916.

VOLUME II

W. Wilkinson Capt.
Comm'd'g 16th Div'l. Cyclist Co.

Original

WAR DIARY

INTELLIGENCE SUMMARY

Army Form C. 2118.

(Erase heading not required.)

Instructions regarding War Diaries and Intelligence Summaries are contained in F. S. Regs., Part II. and the Staff Manual respectively. Title pages will be prepared in manuscript.

Place	Date	Hour	Summary of Events and Information	Remarks and references to Appendices
CITÉ DE VERQUIN	1/2/16		The Company continued work as on 18/1/16, viz:- 50 men at Harley mine entanglement at 36⁵ G26⁵ 3.0. and 36⁵ G26⁵ 3.4.- Remainder at trenches at 36⁵ L24¹ 2.8.	
"	2/2/16		Draft of eight men joined as reinforcements. Nothing to record	
"	3/2/16			
"	4/2/16		L.Cpl. McConville struck off strength of Coy on transfer to Topographical Section.	
"	5/2/16		One man admitted to hospital. One man rejoined from hospital. Nothing to record	
"	6/2/16			
"	7/2/16		Seven men of draft which joined on 27/1/16 struck off strength on transfer to 51st D.C.E.	
"	8/2/16		One man admitted to hospital	
"	9/2/16		One man admitted to hospital	
"	10/2/16		One man rejoined from hospital	
"	11/2/16		2 A.S.C. Drivers and 4 horses attached to Coy for pay and rations.	
"	12/2/16		One man rejoined from hospital. Work on trenches and Harley mine entanglement discontinued. Holiday	
"	13/2/16			
"	14/2/16			
WESTREHEM	15/2/16	1-1.15 P.M.	One man rejoined from hospital. The Company moved to WESTREHEM - map 36⁵ S 24 c.d. and 30 a. arriving 1-1.15 P.M. 2 A.S.C. drivers and 4 horses rejoined their unit.	
"	16/2/16		One man admitted to hospital.	
"	17/2/16		Three men admitted to hospital. The Company was inspected by the Divl. Commander	
"	18/2/16		The Company commenced a course of further training in musketry, bombing, wiring,	
"	19/2/16		Signalling, reconnaissance, etc. Nothing to record	

WAR DIARY
INTELLIGENCE SUMMARY

Army Form C. 2118.

Place	Date	Hour	Summary of Events and Information	Remarks and references to Appendices
WESTREHEM	20/7/16		No 7328 Pte KNEAFSEY - A.M. commissioned as Second Lieutenant in 6th R.Dublin Fus. 3 men rejoined from hospital. - Church Parade were held. -	
"	21/7/16		One man admitted to hospital. - No 6905 Pte Whelan J. appointed unpaid Lance Corporal. Company was inspected by First Corps Commander, who congratulated the C.O. on its general smartness, and its road discipline.	
"	22/7/16		Nothing to record.	
"	23/7/16		One man admitted to hospital.	
"	24/7/16		One man rejoined from hospital.	
"	25/7/16		One man admitted to hospital. - No 6905 Pte Whelan J. appointed L.Cpl. (unpaid)	
"	26/7/16		Nothing to record.	
"	27/7/16			
BUSNES	28/7/16		The company moved to BUSNES. - Map 36b. P2b.d, 27b, 27b, and 27d. - Move completed at 1 P.M. C.Q.M.S. Kearns. D. admitted to hospital.	
"	29/7/16		One man rejoined from hospital.	

SECRET

16 Cyclist
Vol. 3

WAR DIARY
of
16th Divisional Cyclist Company
From 1st March 1916 to 31st March 1916

VOLUME III

[signature]
Lieutenant,
O.C. 16th Div. Cyclist Coy

Army Form C. 2118.

WAR DIARY

~~INTELLIGENCE SUMMARY~~

(Erase heading not required.)

VOLUME III

Instructions regarding War Diaries and Intelligence Summaries are contained in F. S. Regs., Part II. and the Staff Manual respectively. Title pages will be prepared in manuscript.

Place	Date	Hour	Summary of Events and Information	Remarks and references to Appendices
BUSNES	1/3/16		No.2887 Cpl Summers A.P. appointed acting C.Q.M.S., vice C.Q.M.S. Kearns D. No.6905 L/Cpl. Whelan J. appointed paid L/Cpl. No.7841 Pte LeBideau Lce.Cpl. (unpaid) No.7697 Pte Clarence F.A. Permanently attached to A.P.M. as orderly.	
"	2/3/16		One man admitted to hospital. One man rejoined from hospital. No 2171 Pte Forti D. permanently attached to 16th Divl. Company as orderly. Nothing to record.	
"	3/3/16		The Company carried out a reconnaissance of the hands in the new VERQUIN -	
"	4/3/16		VAUDRICOURT - HOUCHIN - NOEUX-les-MINES, and of the hands leading from this area to the section of trenches in the LOOS Salient, and forwarded a report with sketch maps to 16 16th Div. H.Q.	
"	5/3/16		One man rejoined from hospital.	
"	6/3/16		No.6915 L/Cpl. Cronin deprived of lance stripe. A reconnaissance was made of the AIRE - LA BASSÉE Canal from Pt d'ISBERGUES Map 36A. I.33d. 7.3. to BETHUNE, and forwarded report with sketch map, showing condition of tow paths, to 16th Div. H.Q.	
"	7/3/16		Two men admitted to hospital. Nothing to record.	
"	8/3/16			
HURIONVILLE	9/3/16		The Company moved to HURIONVILLE, arriving at 12 noon. One man admitted to hospital.	
"	10/3/16		Nothing to record.	
"	11/3/16			

WAR DIARY
INTELLIGENCE SUMMARY

Army Form C. 2118.

(Erase heading not required.)

Place	Date	Hour	Summary of Events and Information	Remarks and references to Appendices
HURIONVILLE	12/3/16		Nothing to record.	
"	13/3/16		Captain W.H.L. WATSON attached to duty on G.S. 16th Division. Lieutenant H. NEVILLE ROBERTS assumed temporary Command of the Company.	
"	14/3/16		2 men admitted to hospital.	
"	15/3/16		"	
"	16/3/16		3 "	
"	17/3/16		Nothing to record	
"	18/3/16		The Company attended Divine Service. The day was observed as a holiday, and Sports were held in the afternoon. 2 men admitted to hospital. Lieutenant E.U.P. FITZGERALD, 2nd Lieut S. GEDDIS and 11 O.R. attached to 45th Infantry Brigade for instruction in network of Divisional observation post. One man admitted to hospital.	
"	19/3/16		The Company attended Divine Service. 2nd Lieut G.M.E. BAYLY and 10 O.R. reported at Divisional School for Bombing Course. Nothing to record.	
"	20/3/16		One man admitted to hospital.	
"	21/3/16		One man rejoined from hospital. 2 men admitted to hospital One man rejoined from hospital	
"	22/3/16		2 men joined as reinforcements. Lieutenant E.U.P. FITZGERALD, 2nd Lieut S. GEDDIS and 11 O.R. rejoined from 45th Inf. Bde.	
"	23/3/16		Lieutenant G.T. SHAW attached to 15th Div. CYCLISTS, with 14 O.R. for instruction in trench. Maintenance of Communication trenches.	
"	24/3/16		One man rejoined from hospital.	

Army Form C. 2118.

WAR DIARY

INTELLIGENCE SUMMARY

(Erase heading not required.)

Instructions regarding War Diaries and Intelligence Summaries are contained in F. S. Regs. Part II. and the Staff Manual respectively. Title pages will be prepared in manuscript.

Place	Date	Hour	Summary of Events and Information	Remarks and references to Appendices
HURIONVILLE	25/3/16			
"	26/3/16		One man rejoined from hospital. Half Company, under Lieutenant H. Neville Roberts, moved to VAUDRICOURT arriving at 11.30 A.M., and thence proceeded to Communication trenches in relief of 15th Div. CYCLISTS. Relief completed at 8 P.M. Lieutenant E.U.P. FITZGERALD, 2nd Lieut. S. GEDDIS, and 20 O.R. moved to VAUDRICOURT and thence proceeded to the Divisional Observation posts in relief of 15th Div. O.P.s Relief completed by 6 P.M.	
VAUDRICOURT	27/3/16		Remainder of Company, under Lieutenant A.G.F. SIMMS, moved to VAUDRICOURT, arriving at 12 noon.	
"	28/3/16		Work party of 50 O.R. reported to 156th Coy R.E. at PHILOSOPHE at 6.30 P.M. Lieutenant A.G.F. SIMMS and one O.R. granted 9 days leave to U.K.	
"	29/3/16		Work party of 50 O.R. returned from PHILOSOPHE at 6 A.M.	
"	30/3/16		2nd Lieut J. HOGAN and 14 O.R. relieving 14 O.R. in Communication trenches. Work party of 20 O.R. reported to 156th Coy R.E. at PHILOSOPHE at 6 P.M. One O.R. accidentally injured at PHILOSOPHE.	
"	31/3/16		Work party of 20 O.R. returned from PHILOSOPHE at 4 A.M. The Half Company moved from VAUDRICOURT to NOEUX-LES-MINES, arriving at 12 noon. 2 O.R. granted 9 days leave to U.K.	
NOEUX-LES-MINES	"			

16th Cyclo
Vol 4

Confidential
───────────

War Diary
of
16th Divisional Cyclist Company
from 1st April 1916 to 30th April 1916 —

Volume IV.

Minnie Dobbs
Lieutenant,
для Comdg 16th Div. Cyclist Coy.

Army Form C. 2118.

WAR DIARY

INTELLIGENCE SUMMARY.
(Erase heading not required.)

Instructions regarding War Diaries and Intelligence Summaries are contained in F. S. Regs., Part II. and the Staff Manual respectively. Title pages will be prepared in manuscript.

Place	Date	Hour	Summary of Events and Information	Remarks and references to Appendices
NOEUX-LES-MINES	1/4/16		Half Company in NOEUX-LES-MINES relieves half Company in Communication Trenches. Relief completed at 10 P.M. One man admitted to hospital.	
"	2/4/16		2nd Lieut. G.M.E. BAYLY and 10 O.R. returned from Divisional School and rejoined the Coy.	
"	3/4/16		Lieut. E.V.P. FITZGERALD who relieved by Lieut. G.T. SHAW at Divisional Observation Post, and with 20 O.R. reported to O.C. 2nd Line Defences at MAZINGARBE. This party was billeted in MAZINGARBE, and attached to 11th HAMPSHIRE Regt for rations. One man admitted to hospital. Half Company returned from Communication Trenches to NOEUX LES MINES arriving at 1 P.M. This party who not relieved, the work being carried on under other Divisional arrangements. The Company (less parties detached) paraded at Div. Baths House for baths.	
"	4/4/16		Four O.R. joined as reinforcements.	
"	5/4/16		One man returned from hospital.	
"	6/4/16		2nd Lieut. S. GEDDIS and 1 O.R. granted 9 days leave to U.K. Furnished Div. Cmd'rs Guard. Furnished Div. Commander's Guard. One man admitted to hospital.	
"	7/4/16		2 Orderlies attached A.P.M. One orderly attached Signal Coy for telephone duty. The Company carried out a Tactical scheme in training with the Div. Cavalry.	
"	8/4/16		Lieut. A.G.F. SIMMS and one O.R. rejoined from leave. Three O.R. joined as reinforcements. Two shells fell in billeting area of Coy. 3.10 P.M. Church Parades were held. One man rejoined from hospital.	
"	9/4/16		One O.R. rejoined from leave. The Company was inspected by Capt. WATSON at 3 P.M.	
"	10/4/16		The Company Paraded at Div. Baths House for baths.	
"	11/4/16		One man admitted to hospital. 2/Lieut. J. HOGAN reported (shell shock) and on 8/4/16 — Shell which fell in billets area this casualty.	

Army Form C. 2118.

WAR DIARY

INTELLIGENCE SUMMARY

(Erase heading not required.)

Instructions regarding War Diaries and Intelligence Summaries are contained in F. S. Regs., Part II. and the Staff Manual respectively. Title pages will be prepared in manuscript.

Place	Date	Hour	Summary of Events and Information	Remarks and references to Appendices
NOEUX LES MINES	12/4/16		Furnished Div. Commander's Guard. One man admitted to hospital. The Company Carried out a tactical scheme. 2 O.R. granted 9 days leave to U.K. 1 Cycle reports lost. Lieut A.G.F. SIMMS.	
	13/4/16		2 men granted leave to U.K. 2 N.C.Os appointed instructors at Divisional Bombing School. 1 man returned from hospital. The Company ordered to reconnoitre Div area to find suitable places for rifle ranges and bombing grounds. 2/Cpl Chalcroft Palmer and Mansfield promoted Cpls.	
	15/4/16		The Company carried out a tactical scheme with the Div Cavalry. 15 men detailed to learn traffic control.	
	16/4/16		1 O.R. rejoined Company from Signal Company. 2nd Lieut S. Gedche and 1 O.R. returned from leave.	
	17/4/16		2nd Lieut J. Hogan returned to duty from sick list. 15 O.R. detailed to learn Traffic control. 1 O.R. returned from hospital.	
	18/4/16		1 O.R. returned from hospital. Pte Gytt awarded 5 days F.P. No 2. 16 O.R. detailed for Traffic Control. 1 O.R. returned from leave.	
	19/4/16		1 O.R. admitted to hospital	

Army Form C. 2118.

WAR DIARY
or
INTELLIGENCE SUMMARY.
(Erase heading not required.)

Instructions regarding War Diaries and Intelligence Summaries are contained in F. S. Regs., Part II. and the Staff Manual respectively. Title pages will be prepared in manuscript.

Place	Date	Hour	Summary of Events and Information	Remarks and references to Appendices
NOEUX LES MINES.	19-4-16		1 O.R. wounded (Shell fire) and admitted to 33rd C.C.S. 2 O.R. returned from Div. bombing school.	
	20-4-16		Company paraded at Divisional Baths at 10 A.M. 2 minutes Divisional Commander's guard. The Company were paid at 2 P.M. 3 minutes a guard to Divisional detention room	
	21-4-16		2 minutes Divisional Commander's guard and guard at detention room. Church parade for C of E's at 11 A.M. Lieut G. T. Shaw appointed Divisional Rest Officer. Tactical scheme with Divisional Cavalry cancelled on account of bad weather. 2nd Lieut J. Hogan proceeds to MAZINGARBE for duty with D.C. Second Line Defences.	
	22-4-16			
	23-4-16		Lieut A.G.F. SIMMS took over temporary command of Company during absence of C.O. The Company paraded for Church. 3 minutes Detention Guard 16 O.R. detailed for Traffic control.	
	24-4-16		1 O.R. transferred to 12th D.C.C. Lieut E.U.P. FITZGERALD appointed temporary Captain and to command 15th D.C.C. Company paraded for tactical scheme under 2nd Lieut Fedden. 1 O.R. admitted to hospital	
	25-4-16		2 minutes detention Guard and 16 men for traffic control. Company paraded for tactical scheme under 2nd Lieut Fedden. 1 O.R. reported from hospital.	

Army Form C. 2118.

WAR DIARY
or
INTELLIGENCE SUMMARY.
(Erase heading not required.)

Instructions regarding War Diaries and Intelligence Summaries are contained in F. S. Regs., Part II. and the Staff Manual respectively. Title pages will be prepared in manuscript.

Place	Date	Hour	Summary of Events and Information	Remarks and references to Appendices
NOEUX LES MINES.	26-4-16		Furnished detention guard and 16 men for Traffic control. 1 O.R. rejoined from hospital.	
	27-4-16		The Company paraded for a route ride. 2nd Lieut F.E. BUCHANAN reported for duty with the Company. Gas alarm at 5-30 A.M. The Company were ordered to man an alarm post at L 13 a	
	28-4-16		Furnished detention guard and 16 men for Traffic control. Company paraded for baths at 8 A.M.	
	29-4-16		Company paraded for baths and 16 men for Traffic control. Furnished detention guard. Gas alarm at 10 P.M. Company ordered to stand to. Stand to cancelled at 11 P.M. Lieut H.N. ROBERTS and 1 O.R. proceeded on leave to U.K. Gas alarm at 4 A.M. Company ordered to stand to and man alarm post. 1 Officer and 30 O.R. proceeded to trenches to evacuate the guard - 4 men of this party were gassed. 1 N.C.O. and 20 men tee off to report to A.P.M. on the sounding of the gas alarm. Tactical scheme with Divisional Cavalry cancelled.	
	30-4-16		The Company (less men at Observation Posts and orderlies) proceeded to 49th Inf Bgde. H.Q. and thence to Reserve trench. The Company taking portion of reserve trench and supplying fatigue parties to front line etc.	

O.P.S.

SECRET

16 Div
Cyclists
Vol 5

WAR DIARY
of
16th DIVISIONAL CYCLIST COMPANY

From 1st May 1916 to 1st June 1916
(inclusive)

VOLUME V

[signature]
Lieutenant,
for (Capt) Comdg 16th D.C.C.

WAR DIARY

INTELLIGENCE SUMMARY

Army Form C. 2118.

Place	Date	Hour	Summary of Events and Information	Remarks and references to Appendices
NOEUX-LES-MINES	1/5/16		The Company (less observation posts, Divisional orderlies, etc.) attached 46th Inf. Brigade and employed in Reserve Trenches. Company Head Qrs remained at Noeux-les-Mines.	
	2/5/16		do	
	3/5/16		do One O.R. wounded (shrapnel)	
	4/5/16		do	
	5/5/16		do	
	6/5/16		The Company relieved in Reserve Trenches at 4 P.M. and returned to Noeux-les-Mines. Captain W.T.L. WATSON and three O.R. granted leave to U.K.	
	7/5/16		Nothing to record.	
	8/5/16		Inspection of cycles, etc.	
	9/5/16		Inspection of Company in marching order, arms and kit.	
	10/5/16		Lieut. G.T. SHAW granted leave to U.K. also one O.R. One O.R. rejoined from hospital.	
	11/5/16		One O.R. admitted to hospital. Company route ride. Company parades 6.30 P.M. for trench fatigues.	
	12/5/16		Company route ride 9 A.M. Company Parade 6.30 P.M. having been granted extension.	
	13/5/16		One O.R. rejoined from leave, having been granted extension. One O.R. rejoined from leave.	
	14/5/16		One O.R. admitted to hospital. One O.R. rejoined from leave. Company Parade 6.30 P.M. for trench fatigues.	
	15/5/16		2 O.R. admitted to hospital. Company Parade 6.45 P.M. for French fatigues. One O.R. admitted to hospital. Lieut. H.N. ROBERTS rejoined from leave, having been granted extension.	
	16/5/16		2/Lieut. G.M.E. BAYLY and one O.R. granted leave to U.K. 2 O.R. rejoined from leave. One O.R. accidentally wounded. Company parade 6.45 P.M. for French fatigues.	
	17/5/16		One O.R. admitted to hospital. One O.R. rejoined from hospital. Company (less those permanently employed) Paraded 5 P.M. and attached 8th R. Inniskilling Fus. in trenches.	

WAR DIARY

INTELLIGENCE SUMMARY

Army Form C. 2118.

Instructions regarding War Diaries and Intelligence Summaries are contained in F.S. Regs., Part II. and the Staff Manual respectively. Title pages will be prepared in manuscript.

(Erase heading not required.)

Place	Hour, Date	Summary of Events and Information	Remarks and references to Appendices
NOEUX-LES-MINES	18/5/16	Capt. W.H.L. WATSON returned from leave, and continued to be attached D.H.Q. for duty.	
	19/5/16	Nothing to record.	
	20/5/16	Nothing to record.	
	21/5/16	One O.R. admitted to hospital. Lieut. G.T. SHAW and one O.R. rejoined from leave. Shell fell in the Company's billeting area at NOEUX-LES-MINES one of which entered officers billet causing material damage only.	
	22/5/16	2/Lieut. J. HOGAN and 3 O.R. granted leave to U.K. One O.R. admitted to hospital.	
	23/5/16	One O.R. admitted to hospital. One O.R. wounded (at duty)	
	24/5/16	One O.R. killed. 5 O.R. wounded. 2/Lieut. S. GEDDIS admitted to hospital.	
	25/5/16	One O.R. rejoined from leave.	
	26/5/16	2/Lieut. G.M.E. BAYLY rejoined from leave. One O.R. accidentally injured. The Company ceased to be attached to 8th R. Inniskilling Fus. and was attached 7th R. Inniskilling Fus.	
	27/5/16	One O.R. admitted to hospital. One O.R. died of wounds.	
	28/5/16	2 O.R. granted leave to U.K.	
	29/5/16	One O.R. rejoined from hospital.	
	30/5/16	One O.R. admitted to hospital. The Company ceased to be attached to 7th R. Inniskilling Fus., and returned to billets at NOEUX-LES-MINES	
	31/5/16	2 O.R. admitted to hospital. 2/Lt. J. HOGAN rejoined from leave.	
	1/6/16	One O.R. granted leave to U.K. The Company was disbanded on this date and the personnel transferred to Infantry battalions by the 16th Division under authority G.H.Q. No. 6.B./1517 dated 12/5/16	

Forms/C. 2118/10

www.ingramcontent.com/pod-product-compliance
Lightning Source LLC
Chambersburg PA
CBHW081503160426
43193CB00014B/2576